KETCHUP CHIPS

Written by Shelley Anderson

Illustrated by Skyler Langendoen

Copyright 2022 by Shelley Anderson

All rights reserved.

No part of this publication may be reproduced, distributed, or transmitted in any form or by any means, including photocopying, recording, or other electronic or mechanical methods, without the prior written permission of the publisher, except as permitted by U.S. copyright law.

For permission requests, contact Shelley Anderson, Box 39, Rocky Mountain House, Alberta T4T 1A1 or email clearwatercounselling844@gmail.com.

The story, all names, characters, and incidents portrayed in this production are fictitious. No identification with actual persons (living or deceased), places, buildings, and products is intended or should be inferred.

Book Cover and illustrations by Skyler Langendoen

Guide For Parents, Clinicians, and Professionals

Addiction to substances is difficult for adults to understand, let alone children. This book helps children learn about addictions with the support of a trusted adult- how addictions affect people and the ones that love them.

Ketchup Chips is an excellent resource for professionals, parents, and caregivers. Due to the sensitive nature of this topic, it is suggested than an adult, such as a parent or helping professional, read and work through this book with a young person who has been effected by a caregiver's addiction to substances.

Ketchup Chips was written as a response to a therapeutic need to help children of parents/caregivers with substance abuse issues and has been used successfully as a tool to stimulate discussion about addiction. Many children have been able to see themselves and their own experience reflected through Wyatt's story, creating further therapeutic opportunities. Children have stated, "That's just like me."

Join young Wyatt as he struggles to understand his mother's addiction to substances with the help of his play therapist. Wyatt is a very relatable character who responds to his mother's substance abuse issues with confusion, sadness, frustration, and anger. At times he blames himself, and at other times he wonders why he was not enough to make his mom change her behaviour. His therapist, Wendy, helps him to understand his own reactions as well as those of other children experiencing similar difficulties, making it very generalizable to all children.

This book provides a very clear and straightforward narrative for children and adults to understand substance abuse and its effects, as well as the impact of parental substance abuse on children.
My hope is that this book will be an invaluable resource for parents, caregivers, and mental health workers to help children explore and understand the complexities of addictions, their impact on the addicted and the people who love them.

This book is dedicated to all of the kids who have had the courage to share their hurts with me and start on their healing journey.

Hi, my name is Wyatt. I am 10 years old. I am a really fast runner, and I am good at math too. I am not very good at baseball. The Hendersons like baseball, but I don't. They like to go swimming though, and I really like that. I am very brave, and I can do flips off of the rope swing. My brother, Andrew, always claps when I do that. He isn't ready to go off the rope swing because he can't swim a length of the pool yet. I can. Andrew is 8. We live together with the Hendersons. My twin sisters live with us too. They are six years old. I also have an older sister and an older brother. They don't live with us. They live in a different foster home. The Hendersons didn't have enough room for all of us but we get to see my brother and sister for visits sometimes.

We didn't always live in a foster home. We used to live with our Grandma. All of us together. We liked living with her, but it was very crowded because sometimes our cousins stayed with us too.

Now we live with the Hendersons. They are pretty nice. They have two teenage girls, but we don't see them very much because they go to a different school and both of them go to dance class almost every day after school. Sometimes they hang out with us though and watch movies or play games. They also have a dog named Rufus who is super fluffy and loves to be petted. I like Rufus a lot. I think he is my favorite in the whole house.

The social worker said that we will live with the Hendersons until our Mom gets out of "treatment." "Treatment" is a place where people go to stop using alcohol or drugs. I don't know what it is like there, but I hope it is like a spa with a swimming pool and good food to eat. I hope she gets back soon so we can all live together again.

My mom didn't always use alcohol and drugs. Sometimes she was a really good mom, and she took care of us and made food for us and made sure we got up for school. She didn't think we knew about the alcohol, but we did. Sometimes she couldn't get up in the morning and stayed in bed all day, so we didn't go to school. My mom said she was sorry and promised that she would do better, and sometimes she did. But then she would forget to pick us up from school or forget to come to special parent days. I told my teachers that she had the flu or that we had relatives visiting, so she couldn't come. I didn't want them to know about the alcohol. I didn't want them to think that she wasn't a good mom. I didn't want to get taken away from her. One time she did show up to pick us up from school, but she was slurring her words and she didn't make sense and I was really embarrassed, so I stopped telling her about school events, and told her to stop coming to pick us up, that we could walk home by ourselves. I told her that I would take care of Andrew and the twins.

I didn't understand why my mom had to drink. Sometimes she said that we were too much and that she was really stressed so we tried to behave better. But there was always something that made her want to drink. Sometimes my mom said mean things to us, but I knew she didn't really mean it. Sometimes I was glad when she would fall asleep on the couch but then I would get really scared if I couldn't wake her up to ask what we were going to have for supper. Sometimes we didn't have supper.

Then a social worker came and talked to us at school. I told her that everything was fine and that my mom took good care of us. She must not have believed me because, that night, we all went to stay at my Grandma's.

Now we are at the Hendersons. Me and Andrew share a room and we stick together. Mostly it's okay. I miss my mom and my Grandma and the rest of my family, but I am glad Andrew and the twins are here. There's lots to do and I even have fun, but sometimes I get really mad and fight with everyone, even Andrew. I don't even know why I get so mad. I just can't help it. When Mrs. Henderson asks me what made me so mad, I make something up, but the truth is, sometimes my feelings are just really messy, like a big tangle of string, and I can't figure it out.

Once, after I got really mad at the twins, Mrs. Henderson said that I was going to see a counsellor to help me with my feelings. I was really nervous at first because I didn't know what a counsellor was, and I didn't like to talk about my feelings.

The counsellor's name was Wendy and she seemed nice. She gave me hot chocolate that tasted like a melted chocolate bar. And she had a really cool room with lots of different toys to play with. Sometimes she had some ideas of fun things to do and sometimes I got to choose the activity. She had a cool sand tray with a whole bunch of little animals and people to go in it, even dragons! We played balloon badminton and made things with clay. When it was my turn to choose the activity, I always chose Lego. At the end, she always read a book to me.

It was fun to go visit Wendy. We played a lot but sometimes we talked too. She helped me to understand some things about my mom's problem with alcohol and drugs. It is called "addiction." I don't totally understand it all yet, but she explained that addiction can be because of a chemical problem in the brain. Or it could be a genetic problem that is passed down in families like the color of your eyes or the color of your hair. It could also be because of personal problems like when people have lots of stress because they can't find a job or are having problems with someone in their lives, like their husband or wife.

She said that scientists and doctors don't even totally understand it all. I thought to myself, if they can't even understand it, then how can a kid understand it?!

I learned that lots of people drink alcohol or take drugs to feel better. Some of the people don't have personal problems, but some do. The alcohol or drugs makes them feel better or more relaxed for a while or else they do it to have fun. Sometimes they just don't want to feel their own feelings and the alcohol or drugs makes them forget about bad things or makes them feel nothing at all and they like that. Some people can drink alcohol or take drugs once in a while, but some people have a hard time stopping. This is addiction. It means they have a hard time stopping, even when bad things happen because of it. It is so confusing! Why do they keep drinking even when bad things start to happen, like their kids get taken away? I try to imagine not being able to stop doing something that did bad things to you. Sometimes I hold up a piece of candy or something really tasty and tell myself that I am not allowed to eat it, just to see if I could stop myself. It depends on what kind of candy it is, ha-ha. If it is ketchup chips, I know for sure I am going to give in. I love love love ketchup chips and could have them for breakfast, lunch, and supper. Maybe that's what it is like for my mom, the alcohol is like ketchup chips.

I also wonder a lot about what alcohol feels like. Like what does my mom like about it? It looks fun sometimes but other times it doesn't look fun at all. Wendy said that alcohol is a drug, and it affects the body and the brain. It changes people's feelings and how they act. They may feel dizzy, silly, happy, or free to act however they want.

They may feel out of control, angry, violent, sad, tired, and like throwing up. I think that is true. Sometimes my mom is super fun and silly when she is drinking. She dances around when she is cooking. She laughs and laughs and sometimes spins us around and dances with us. My older brother and sister don't think this is fun. They always got mad and left the house. I liked it when my mom was funny and laughed.

But sometimes she would get grumpy and say mean things and I would take my little brother and the twins outside or to our rooms.

And the worst was when she would sleep on the couch and I couldn't wake her up. Sometimes I took the bottles of alcohol and hid them away, hoping she would not find them, but she always did. I wanted to help her but I didn't know how. She said that she could quit drinking anytime, but then why didn't she?

Sometimes I was so confused that I didn't even know what I was feeling, and it all came out as anger. I wanted to hit and break things and not even care what happened. And then I would just feel like crying. Wendy said that all of these feelings are normal. She said that many kids, just like me, with a parent who has trouble with addictions feel all kinds of different feelings. Just like me, they feel worried and scared, they get sad and then angry and hate everyone. Sometimes they feel embarrassed and ashamed. Just like me, sometimes they feel like their mom doesn't love them enough to stop drinking the alcohol, like she loves drinking more than she loves her kids! Sometimes I think that if we didn't cause her so much stress that she wouldn't have to drink so much. Wendy said that this isn't true, and I want to believe her, but it's hard.

When I get really sad and mad, I try to remember what Wendy told me. That it's not my fault that my mom has a problem with drinking alcohol and that I can't make her stop. I hope that the people at the Treatment Center can make her better so she can come home and our whole family can be together again. Wendy said that some people can learn to drink less or stop drinking completely, but some people find it really hard and that it may take a long time to change. I think this is true because my mom did stop drinking for awhile sometimes, but she always started again. I learned that this is called a relapse and that it is often part of getting better. I told Wendy that I was scared my mom would die because of drinking. She agreed that this was a very big feeling for a little person to have.

Sometimes I worry that I will have addictions some day too, especially when I think about how hard it is to resist ketchup chips. I think my older brother already has a problem with drugs and that really scares me. Wendy said that there are some things that I can do to help make sure that I don't have a problem with addictions when I get older. She said that it is important for me to have my own goals and dreams too, and to just be a kid. She said that I need to find things that I enjoy doing, to help me cope with big feelings. I try to have fun and not to worry so much about my mom. Turns out that is a hard thing to do but I am going to keep trying.

Wendy helped me figure out some things that help me to feel better when I am really upset. I made a list of them and put it on the wall beside my bed. Then, when I am upset, I can go to the list and almost always find something that helps. Some of the things I can do all by myself, like punch my pillow or go for a walk or do jumping jacks. Sometimes I crawl under my covers and feel safe and warm. Sometimes I draw or play with lego. And sometimes I eat ketchup chips! But mostly I try to save them for a special treat. I also learned that sometimes I can't change my feelings all by myself and I need help from someone else. So I ask Andrew if he wants to go play outside or I go to the kitchen and Mrs. Henderson figures out that I might need to be around her for awhile. That's when she might ask me to help her make supper.

I act like I don't really want to be there but actually I do and I am glad she gives me a job to do so I can be with her until I am feeling better. Sometimes I even just go pet the dog, Rufus, for awhile until the feeling goes away. I'm glad they have a dog and not a goldfish. Oh yeah, that's another thing that Wendy taught me, big feelings come and go, like waves. The waves come in and go out. I know that even if it is a big wave, it will go back out eventually, so I just need to learn how to surf my feelings better!

I sure hope my mom gets better soon but I know now that it can take a long time and that it's important for me to be in a safe place while she is getting better. I still wish that I could help her somehow. Like I said, I get so worried sometimes that she might die because of alcoholism. Now THAT is a really big feeling and I am not that good of a surfer yet. When I get that feeling, I almost always need help from someone to feel better. Wendy helped me to understand that I didn't cause my mom's addiction and I can't control it or cure it, but I can be somewhere safe while she is trying to get better. And, most importantly, I can remember that she loves me and I love her.

With Wendy's help, I made a long list of things that help me to feel better when I am upset. I added some extra ones to share with you. Some of the things can be done all by yourself and some need help from another person. If you have a hard time with big feelings sometimes like me, then maybe you could try some of these ideas, or add some of your own. I hope that learning about addiction has helped you like it has helped me. And then, who knows? Maybe you could help another kid!

THINGS THAT HELP

- PET MY DOG OR CAT
- GO FOR A WALK
- LISTEN TO MUSIC
- DRAW OR COLOUR
- CLIMB A TREE
- SING OR HUM
- PLAY A BOARD GAME
- WATCH A MOVIE
- PLAY WITH A FRIEND OR SIBLING
- BAKE COOKIES
- HAVE A BATH OR SHOWER
- WRITE DOWN WHAT'S BOTHERING ME
- SHOOT BASKETS
- GO FOR A BIKE RIDE
- CRY
- WIRTE A STORY
- CLEAN MY ROOM

- READ A BOOK
- BRETH SLOWLY IN AND OUT
- LOOK AT PHOTOS
- PLAY A VIDEO GAME
- DANCE
- BE ALONE FOR A WHILE
- HANG AROUND WITH OTHERS
- GO FOR A RUN
- MOW THE LAWN
- SKRIBBLE ON A PIECE OF PAPER
- RIP UP SOME PAPER
- YELL INTO A PILLOW OR PUNCH IT
- CALL A FRIEND
- MAKE A SONG
- BE KIND TO MYSELF
- FEEL MY FEELINGS
- TURN THE MUSIC UP LOUD
- GO OUTSIDE
- WATCH THE CLOUDS

ABOUT THE AUTHOR

Shelley Anderson is a Clinical Social Worker living and working in rural Alberta, Canada for the past 30 years, working with children and families from a trauma and attachment framework. Her clients have taught her so much about resilience and our innate desire to heal.

Shelley is now using that knowledge to write the books she would have liked to have had over the years as tools to educate and support. Her hope is that children will be able to relate to the characters and see themselves in the books she has written, providing deeper understanding about difficult subjects, as well as decreasing stigma and shame.

In addition, they may also be helpful to the adults in their lives to help them better understand the impact of experiences such as sexual abuse, addiction, and attachment injury.

Website Address: https://getouttheretoo9.wixsite.com/clearwater-books

ABOUT THE ILLUSTRATOR

Skyler Langendoen is a multi-talent, self-taught artist and illustrator who currently resides in Banff, Alberta.

Skyler does a beautiful job bringing this story to life and helping readers connect with this difficult subject matter in a meaningful way.

Samantha is a young girl who loves dance and has a corn snake named Boots. Life changes for Sam when her uncle comes to live with them and sexually abuses her, leaving her very confused and full of conflicted feelings. The abuse stops when Sam discloses the abuse to her school teacher and, even though life seems to get back to normal, Sam loses interest in activities she previously loved and her happy demeanour changes.

When Sam starts to see a therapist, she begins to understand her response to the sexual abuse, how it has affected her, and how it affects other kids. Join Sam as she seeks to understand this difficult experience and work through it with the help of her therapist and her family.

While this is a difficult subject, it is important that children who have experienced childhood sexual abuse can see themselves and their responses in the characters of a book. This helps to decrease the shame and stigmatization, better allowing them to move beyond the experience and start the healing process.

Olive is a tiny black and white kitten that has to leave her family. She goes to live in a home with a young girl named Katie. Olive is very scared and not prepared to trust Katie and the others in the house.

Although it is difficult at first, eventually Katie and the furry cast of characaters in the house help Olive to begin to settle in to the new family and trust again.

This is a story about loss and attachment. Join Olive as she learns that it is okay to trust and to feel safe again.

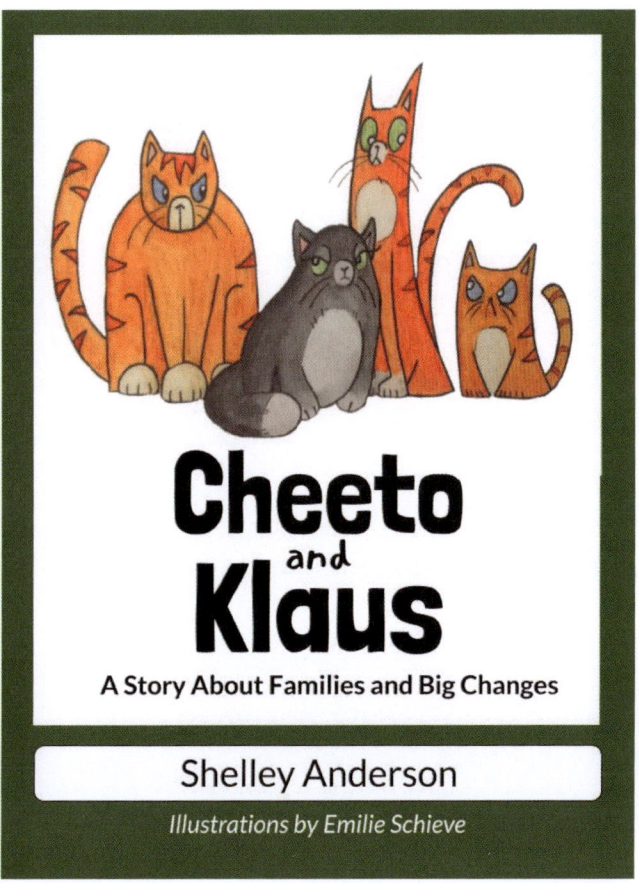

Two young cats move in with a new family after suffering neglect in their previous home. The new family already has two cats, who are not sure that they are prepared to have Cheeto and Klaus move in.

The family goes through many difficulties as they try to figure out if they can be a family with four cats.

This is a story about families going through big changes all of the accompanying emotions. As you will see, things do not go smoothly, but the family decides that they have enough room in their hearts and their home for the new family members.

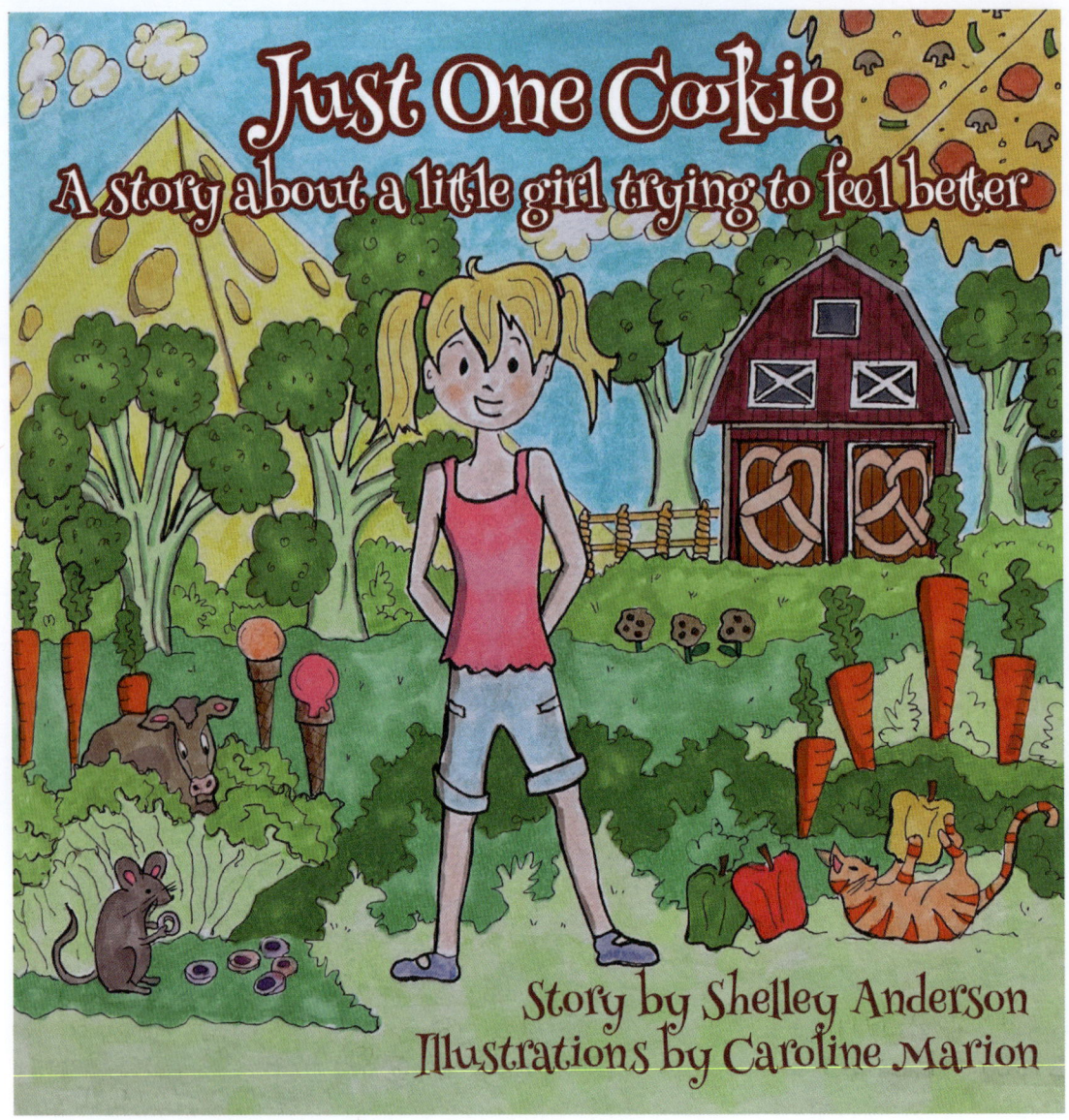

Sometimes we can feel a little bit empty, wanting to fill up on all the wrong things, just to feel better. That might be food, toys, time, or attention. But it never feels like enough. This seems especially true for kids that have had difficult histories. The result can often be that kids feel frustrated and continue seeking, while the adults around them feel overwhelmed and ashamed that they cannot meet the child's needs adequately.

This is the story of a little girl who tries to fill herself up with food, but cannot get enough. When, in her imagination, she consumes everything in the house, the whole neighbourhood, the planet, and starts on the solar system, she realizes that things are getting out of control.

That's when her wise grandmother suggests that maybe that's not what she needs. Perhaps the void she is trying to fill is best filled with a warm, nurturing, safe relationship. When the little girls allows herself to be nurtured and taken care of, she starts to feel a little less empty.

Printed in Great Britain
by Amazon